A Spring to Remember

Luci Hoffman

Identifiers:

ISBN: 979-8-9913590-8-5 (paperback)

979-8-9913590-9-2 (e-book)

Library of Congress Control Number 2025918238

Book cover design: Lucinda Hoffman

Book cover photo: Lucinda Hoffman

Published by
Never Alone Publishing
Fort Wayne, IN

Never Alone
PUBLISHING

Dedicated to the memory of my mother,

Donna Mae Grant Bradford Webster

Who encouraged me daily,
Loved me unconditionally,
And taught me, by example,
How to live a Godly life.

A Spring to Remember

"Just when you think you've forgotten it all
A fleeting thought, a word, a name will recall
A memory from childhood propelling you back in time.
Come with me and I'll share some of mine."

Reflections of a Midwest farmer's daughter expressed
through poems, short stories, and pictures by
Lucinda (Luci) Hoffman.

Included in this book are stories, poems and muses written
by Donna Webster and Martha Webster Rust.

Contents

The Farm

The Family

Final Thoughts

The Farm

A Spring to Remember

I was born in the spring. I'm not referring to the season of the year. My actual month of birth is January. I am referencing the feelings I experienced when reflecting on my youth.

My first recollection places me in a rocking chair with my older sister, Martha Ann, on the enclosed porch of our farmhouse in Ohio. Since she was only eighteen months my senior, we had no trouble sharing a seat in the sturdy wood rocking chair. I was two years old.

I remember my great uncle John holding me in his lap, reading to me in that same chair. He was a kind and gentle man, a carpenter by trade and a farmer.

Many hours were spent sitting with Uncle John in the shade watching him carve things out of sticks. I couldn't tell you what he carved. He would search diligently under the trees until he found just the right twig. He sharpened his pocketknife and "whittled" to his heart's content, pausing only to knock the ashes out of his pipe and refill it with fresh tobacco. Striking the match on the metal arm of the glider sent an acidic odor into the air, which was quickly replaced by the pungent smell of cherry tobacco.

We didn't talk. We just sat there "pondering" and enjoying the shade and the quiet. He had never married. I always wondered why. He would have been a wonderful father and husband. My mother told me a girl broke his heart when he was younger, and he never fell in love again.

Uncle John's brother, Jim, and his wife, Annie, lived one mile away in a wonderful Victorian farmhouse built by the two brothers. Uncle John would take me there to visit. I loved to help feed and water the large, blind workhorses, hold the kittens, and play with the puppies. I remember playing for hours with small, red fireplace bricks in the spacious attic and was always treated with fresh honey and honeycomb on homemade bread upon leaving. Uncle John died in his sleep at eighty-two.

My great-grandmother, Martha Etta, had been widowed early in her marriage, and, like her brother, John, chose to remain single. She had one child, Richard. Grandma Webster was tiny in stature but presented a formidable presence. She had tuberculosis and hardening of the arteries and spent most of her later years inside the house. She had endured a hard life on the farm. Her husband died from tuberculosis one year after they married. He was twenty-two. Their child, Richard, was three days old.

Although Martha showed great impatience with, and intolerance for, children, she often invited me into her room to share a piece of her hidden stash, pink peppermint lozenges. She had some quirks that drove my mother crazy. She would stuff the pockets of her cotton robe full of little folded squares of toilet paper. "You never know when you might need to blow your nose," she said when questioned about it. She often fell asleep in her chair, snoring loud enough to wake the dead. Mom would say, "Why don't you go to bed?" to which she would reply, "I'm not asleep. I'm just resting my eyes." Great-Grandma Webster died in her sleep at ninety-one.

My grandfather, Richard, had married twice. His first wife, Margaret, passed away from consumption when my father, Charles, and his younger sister, Dorothy, were four and two years of age, respectively. Richard and his second wife, Mae Lee, had two children, Aunt Betty and Uncle Billy. Richard died in an auto accident at the age of forty.

After their father's death, Charlie and Dorothy remained on the farm with Great-Grandma Webster. Mae Lee and her two children moved two miles away to Dixon, Ohio. Mae Lee took over Richard's duties at the post office and became one of the first female postmistresses in the state of Ohio.

My father, Charles Eugene Webster, was a very industrious worker. He was an engineer at Panhandle Eastern Pipeline Company, ran a small motor repair shop from home, and farmed one hundred and twenty acres "on the side." My fondest memories of my dad during my youth revolved around the hours we shared working on the farm together, sharing a Chocolo or orange soda at the local grain elevator, repairing machinery in the machine shop (he repaired, I watched), and walking a mason jar of ice water across the field to him as he drove the tractor on a hot summer day. My dad was also a talented musician. He couldn't read a note of music, but he could play many instruments including the banjo, guitar Hawaiian guitar, the piano, and the harmonica. He sang bass in a men's gospel quartet. I have cherished recollections of nights spent around the piano listening to the quartet or tapping my foot to the music.

My mother, Donna Mae Grant Bradford Webster, often seemed overwhelmed with responsibility—four children, her husband's ailing grandmother, an elderly uncle, a niece that she babysat, farm chores, and a husband who worked two jobs and farmed. I often wonder how she managed it all.

Milking the cows twice a day, raising and butchering chickens to earn a little extra money, canning vegetables, and answering phone calls for Dad's repair shop. Mother drove the tractor and worked on the farm, cultivating, discing, and plowing. She was a city girl and knew little about farm life until she married Charlie. That's a story for another time.

Life on a farm is extremely hard but rewarding. There were plenty of chores to go round. My older sister, two younger brothers, and I spent countless hours weeding and harvesting the two-acre garden, mowing the yard, hauling manure, helping in the fields, feeding the livestock, and gathering eggs, but there was also time for playing. We played in the woods, at the bridge, in the creek, in the barn, in the milk house, in the pump house, in the trees, in the attic, in the chicken coop, in the corn crib, in the hopper wagon, at the neighbor's house—anywhere a kid could go. We played as hard as we worked. Everything was new. Everything was exciting. Life was wonderful.

Then spring turned into summer. High school years were upon me. Life's challenges seemed to shift from physical to mental and emotional. Schoolwork was simple for me. I had inherited my dad's engineering abilities and my mother's artistic skills. The combination provided the necessary tools to meet the mental challenges of high school head on. Confronting the emotional challenges was difficult.

I had my share of interested male friends—the boy next door, the kid at church, the summer fling at the lake, the kissing cousin, the local hood—you know, the usual sampling of suitors. Then, HE appeared. The one who stole my heart. HE rode in on his motorcycle with the "kissing cousin" in tow. We had on matching Henley shirts, the kind with no collar and five or six buttons on the front. It had to be a sign. He lived four miles away in Adams County. How did this nice, handsome, virile guy live so close, and I did not know it? Where had he been all my life? Why did the sky suddenly seem bluer? The grass greener? The world a bigger place?

The next four years were a blur of motion and emotion. Drive-ins, theaters, pizza parlors, bowling alleys, motorcycle rides, basketball games. This was overwhelming for a little country girl who barely got off the farm. Along with all this worldly exposure were the demands at an emotional level.

What did I believe in? What were my moral standards? How far should we go before marriage? Should I worry about that girl that keeps chasing him at ballgames? Should I date other guys? Should we marry? If we do, will he be true? Am I ready to make such a commitment? Am I ready to be a parent? The world was full of questions. I thought some were answered when I said, "I do."

We restored and moved into a house that his parents owned. Our daughter, Angie, was born eighteen months after we were married. Farm life, something I was familiar with, was again the center of my life. Mowing yards, feeding the livestock, milking the cows, cleaning the barn, bailing hay, and canning the garden produce had a familiar feel to it. It was a joyous time, or so I thought.

The strange thing about fall is that it creeps up on you silently. The trees are green and full of life and then, without warning, you notice discoloring and decay setting in. How could things change so quickly? One day the world was full of sunshine and flowers and warmth, the next day it was overcast with doubt and fear. Days that should provide fulfillment and reward were now shadowed by physical and emotional abuse—drugs, drinking, other women, lies, not knowing where he was, not knowing who he was with, not being able to trust the one person you thought you could put your trust in. These are the signs of the coming winter. You can try to ignore the signs, but it won't change the outcome. Winter was well on its way.

Winter. Cold and gray. Lifeless. Webster describes it as "a period of inactivity or decay." It's close to death, but you can't be dead, or you wouldn't feel the cold so much. Do what you must do to get by. Work, walk, talk, eat, but don't think. Thinking hurts too much. Sleep. Close your mind to the cold. Close your eyes to the ugliness of it. Pull the covers over your head. Shut out the world.

I tried. I tried to shut out the world. I took the coldness of winter inside to numb the pain. I questioned my ability to be loved and my moral standards. I wondered if I could ever love or trust again. I felt the pain of rejection and wanted it to stop. I would stop it. I would bury my feelings so deeply that nothing could reach them. Nothing could make me feel again. Nothing!

Except, memories of spring. While buried in my "period of inactivity and decay," thoughts crept through the fog. Thoughts I had tried to bury. Thoughts that might make me feel again, which was something I didn't want to do. Thoughts of that first spring of my life.

The farm—warm sunshine on my face, warm animal smells in the barn, warm hands holding me in a rocking chair, warm eggs from a warm nest, warm honey on hot homemade bread, warm freshly tilled dirt sifting through my fingers, everything warm. No matter how hard I tried to shut out the sun, the warmth had a way of infiltrating every small crevice it could find. Perhaps spring, new and refreshing, could breathe life into this cold heart.

It was time to do a little spring cleaning. Open the windows of my soul and let the fresh air in. Clear the cobwebs from my brain and look at life from a new perspective. Out with the old and in with the new. A new house, a new job, and, eventually, a new husband and new beginnings.

My life, since that first "year," has seen many seasonal changes. Some were short and not too memorable. Others were longer, often painful. And some, like the "dog days of summer," were times you wish you could capture forever. As I look back upon that first cycle of seasons in my life, I realize it was an inaugural into life's many seasonal changes. I now accept, and even look forward to, the changes in my life. God, in his infinite wisdom, knew that the warmth of summer is best appreciated by feeling the coldness of winter, and that the death and decay of fall are necessary to cherish the rebirth of spring. I thank God for allowing me to experience spring as my first season. I pray I may give my children and grandchildren a spring to remember.

Martha Ann (3 years old)
Lucinda Sue (1 1/2 years old)
Great-Uncle John

The Barn

You beckon to me with doors open wide,
Yearning to share the secrets inside.
Stories you hold within those old walls
Come to surface as my mind recalls
Memories of childhood, long, long ago.

Times and events long past, even so
It seems only yesterday I played
Building forts and tunnels in the hay
Oblivious to the mold and decay,
The itching, the sneezing, the heat of the day.

The courage it took to climb to the top and jump in the oat
bin with a flop.
The racing of my heart in my chest
When crossing ledges so narrow, and yet
It felt so good to be defying death.

Animal noises from musty stalls
The pigs, the cows, the chickens, and all.
The smell of fresh milk and harvest of grain
Breathes life into an empty wood frame.
Will you ever see such life again?

A stolen kiss in the haymow that year,
Swinging from ropes and pulleys in fear,
The day the neighbor kid stepped on a nail,
Pretending not to hear Mom when she yelled.
And doing what we promised "never to tell!"

Look at your doors, hanging by a thread
And your roof's partly gone, unfixable I dread.
You stand empty, solemn, looking forlorn.
Your paint is faded. Your shutters are torn.

Memories of yesteryear are all that's allowed.
Of times when you stood noble and proud
When you were cherished for what you could hold.
Now you're remembered for stories untold.

So, with a mixture of love for what you were,
And regret for what you're not,
I bid you farewell, my childhood friend.

The Ground Hogs

By Donna Mae Webster (1994)

June this year is extremely hot, 98 degrees in the shade. In the fall, the Amish are coming to raise the barn and put a new foundation under it. The barn will have to be cleaned out so that they can "find" the walls. Charlie and I have our work cut out for us. Since we are only home from Sunday evening to Wednesday mornings (lake life), we will have to spend at least one day a week cleaning the barn. Two of the grandchildren are helping us on Monday.

We discovered there are at least seven groundhogs living under the concrete floor at the south end of the barn. Every morning and evening, they sneak out to eat. First, the babies poke their heads out, followed by the adults. Something must be done. Groundhogs are very destructive.

It was during this time that the neighbor's German shepherd came to visit Andrea and Matthew, followed by "mama cat." The cat left and came back with two gray kittens.

David has several guns, so I called him to assist with the groundhog problem. He and Deb brought a twenty-two semi-automatic rifle over. It holds eighteen bullets.

David shot at one of the groundhogs and missed.

Between the kids, the dog, the cat, and the kittens, it was beginning to feel like a circus around here. Charlie and David headed for the north end of the barn so they could get a better aim on the ornery critters.

Just as David was taking aim, the neighbor drove in the driveway and parked in front of the barn, between David and the groundhog. He had come to reclaim his dog, his cat, her kittens, and a couple heads of cabbage from Charlie's garden.

Charlie shot one more groundhog on Saturday.

On Sunday, when we came home from church, there was a large groundhog sitting in front of the barn door. Charlie yelled, "Stop the car. I'll sneak into the garage, get the gun, and shoot it." I told him I thought it looked like it was already dead, but he shot it anyway. As it turned out, David had shot the groundhog earlier and propped it up on a stick to make it look like it was praying.

All the groundhogs are now dead or have decided to find a new home. We are now the caretakers of four kittens, three gray ones and one black one. I called the neighbor and told him he owes us "kitty support."

Remodeling of the Barn

By Donna Mae Webster (1995)

John J. Jones (b: 1874, d:1957) built the barn in the early 1900s. It served many purposes. The work horses, Pearl and Rex, were housed there along with the family's milk cows. It held hogs and baby pigs which were raised for meat and to sell. We stayed up many nights delivering litters of baby pigs, plugging in heat lamps, and bedding the stalls with clean straw. Later, three-day-old calves were purchased at the cattle barn auction to be raised as steers for added income.

The Amish put a new foundation under the barn and the big doors on the back were removed and a solid wall took its place. During haymaking time, the loose hay was layered in the hayloft with a big fork and sprinkled with salt to keep it from spoiling. Grandma Martha Jones Webster sent her brother, John, to the attic to get salt. It was stored in a lard can next to the sugar. John grabbed the sugar by mistake.

During World War II, sugar was rationed. Any extra was stored until needed. The family laughed about it later, but it was a serious thing at the time. The horses and cows thought the hay was exceptionally good that year. Eventually, we bought a hay baler and stacked the bales of hay in the north hayloft and bales of straw in the south hayloft. The hay fork still hangs up high by the barn roof on the inside of the barn.

A third floor was installed, and water was piped to a brooder room. Chickens were raised on this floor for many years. The haylofts have straight ladders, so there was room to build steps to access the third floor. They had no railing.

When we quit raising animals, the barn became storage for machinery, the old flat wagon, the box frame of the old Studebaker wagon, wagon wheels, horse collars, and pop and whiskey bottles from long ago.

In the south hayloft was stored iron kettles, chicken cages, feeders and waterers, the pump jack from the early water system in the house, Model A car parts, and more.

When Uncle John died in 1957, Charlie and Donna inherited half of the farm and bought the other half from Charlie's sister, Dorothy. The idea to remodel the barn was born in 1994. It became a reality in 1995.

Great-Uncle John helped raise Charles Webster after his father died. When the Webster children, Martha Ann, Lucinda Sue, John Charles, and David Eugene, were growing up, they spent many hours playing in the barn. On any rainy day you could find them and their friends there. They dug tunnels in the haymow, walked across the plank from the north side hayloft to the south side hayloft. They would climb to the third-floor chicken pen and shoot basketballs.

You could hear them laughing as they jumped into the soybean bin. One time, Cindy and cousin Kathy tried to build a fire (probably to cook for their dolls) and almost burned the barn down. Luckily, the fire went out and caused no damage. It was several years before I found out about that episode.

July 12, 1995. An Amish crew came to start work on the barn. Emanuel Miller from near Monroe, IN, is the crew leader. They cut two feet from the bottom of the barn at the north and east sides to the south side of the double doors (east side), raised the barn, tore out old concrete, and poured new footers. Tomorrow they will pour the concrete foundation. Mr. Miller and Sons and Mr. Hawkins took down the big east side doors and closed them in.

July 21, 1995. Just came home from the lake. Been there since Tuesday. Mr. Miller has all the footers and foundation done. I cannot believe it. I am impressed. They work so hard.

July 27, 1995. The barn is finished! Mr. Miller and his crew left at 12:40 p.m. It looks great! There's a lot of work yet to do. We will hire someone to haul the old concrete away and bring in some topsoil. The neighbors, Schlemmer's, took some of the concrete to fill in washouts along the creek.

Uncle John Jones, Richard Webster, Pearl, and Rex

My Shelter

I long for the shelter of your embrace
When solace from life I seek.
You hide me in your shadows.
And strengthen me when I'm weak.

I run to you in unblinded faith,
Knowing you'll always be there,
To share my unspoken
secrets, and hear my every care.

You've watched me grow in so many ways.
And have patiently been my friend.
Dolls, tea parties, building
Forts, our excursions had no end.

You encouraged dreams of tomorrow.
Yet, celebrated each day.
Touching all that surrounds
You in your own unique way.

Oh, glorious oak, you wondrous tree.
We called you, "The Party Tree."
I can't help but feel that God had his
Hand in planting you there just for me!

The Party Tree

DIXON M. E. CHURCH, DIXON, O.

The Little Country Church

The Little Country Church

There's something that draws me near to you,
I'm not sure what it is.
But when your steeple comes into view
my eyes begin to mist.

To see you now, it's hard to imagine.
That once you nobly stood.
Welcoming those who sought your Shelter,
Desiring to worship God.

Your stained-glass windows are old and cracked.
Your paint is faded and worn.
The shingles on your unkempt roof
are missing or sorely torn.

I can't resist entering your gates once more,
drawn to relive the past.
The people I loved, the things I learned,
It went by all too fast.

The door creaks as I cross the threshold,
The hinges are rusty with age.
The smell of mildew tickles my nose.
Dust filters down through the haze.

I stand in awe as the sanctuary.
Transforms before my eyes.
Instead of seeing dusty pews,
I envision people starting to rise.

With hymnals in hand, they invoke their Lord.
They lift their hearts in song.
It seems so real, those glorious hymns,
That I almost started singing along.

My eyes move to the front of the room
as to the altar I gaze.
Where one might see wood, worn with age
I see people bowing in praise.

The place on the wall where His Cross once hung,
Still shadows its figure yet.
Reminding that once Christ touches your life,
You never truly forget.

And, as I turn to leave this place,
I'm reminded of this verse again.
"God does not live inside these walls,
But in the hearts of men."

The Bridge

The muddy water rippled around twigs and rocks, winding its way down the creek. Lying back on the sun-dried bank, I watched the clouds as they slowly crept across the blue sky, feeling the touch of a soft breeze on my face and the warmth of the sunshine in my hair. It was a lazy day in late August on our small midwestern farm. The morning chores finished, Mom allowed us to sneak away to the creek for a few minutes of fun. Her usual warning of "Don't get muddy!" floated on the breeze and whipped away.

The freedom of being out from under Mom's ever-watchful eye was exhilarating. My older sister, Marty, my younger brother, John, and I danced down the stretch of stone road leading to "the bridge." The bridge was our special place, a secret place of dream weaving and play-acting.

A certain ritual was involved when going to the bridge. The transformation from reality to pretend had to be done gradually—like the shedding of one skin and the donning of another.

We stopped on top of the bridge and dropped stones into the water, trying to hit the leaves that floated by. John bravely climbed up the metal trellis high above the creek and, daring life to make him miss a step or lose his balance, slowly inched his way across the bridge. A look of total triumph crossed his face as he jumped to the pavement on the other side.

A mulberry bush marked the worn path that wound its way under the bridge to the base of the creek. You couldn't pass that bush without grabbing a handful of those juicy berries. I'm not sure whether it was the taste of the berries that drew me to the bush or the pretense that, once eaten, I would become someone other than myself. Someone from another place and time. Someone who lived a life of excitement and intrigue.

Sometimes we would be pirates exploring a deserted island looking for buried treasure. Sometimes we would be military men hiding behind shrubs while enemy forces searched the bank for survivors. Other times we would pretend we were pioneers, catching our daily supply of fresh fish, crawdads, and turtles. Mostly we would catch crawdads. On one occasion Marty caught a snake. She was fishing with the neighbor boy's new fishing pole. That was also the day we pretended to be scuba divers seeking lost treasure. We never found it.

The transition back to reality usually included a dip in the creek. Someone would "accidentally" slip into the water during one of our journeys and, before long, everyone was sliding down the muddy bank into the cool depths. Floating bugs and debris were totally ignored, as were the thoughts of crawdads biting our toes, leeches clinging to our bodies, or snakes swimming past our legs. All that mattered was that we were having fun.

The sound of the car horn sharply brought us back to reality. That was our signal to come home. Mom usually greeted us with a cold shower at the outdoor pump. It was hard to convince her that "we" weren't muddy. The mud belonged to an Indian who had to jump in to save his drowning friend, or to a pirate who had to swim to safety after his ship sunk.

The bridge has since been replaced by a new structure. The metal trellis gave way to two new shiny guardrails, and the bushes that lined the creek bank were bulldozed to allow for better water flow. But the bridge from reality to pretend still lingers in my memory. The pretense of being anyone you want to be gave way to the reality that you can do anything you set your mind to—and, when my kids ask if they can go the creek, I smile knowingly and call after them with tongue in cheek… "Don't get muddy!"

The Walk-In Attic

By Donna M. Webster (1960)

At the top of the stairs and to the right of the landing is one of my favorite places—the walk-in attic.

Uncle John Jones and his brother, Jim, built our house in 1906. The attic played a significant role in the family's lives. It not only provided storage for unused odds and ends, but it was a perfect environment to keep salt, flour, walnuts, and other dry goods. Two wires running the length of the attic provided a drying place for clothes during the winter. The clothes would "freeze dry" as there is no heat in the attic except for the warmth that radiates from the chimney stack which is located on the west wall next to the small entrance door. At the east end of the attic is a small window which provides light year-round and ventilation in the summer.

As you stand on the landing outside of the attic looking in, you are in the present. Upon opening the small door, ducking your head, and stepping down into the attic, you are transported into the past.

There is an aisle with a red strip of carpeting down the middle of the room. Items are stored on both sides. You can stand up straight in the center of the room if you are under four feet tall. The roof slopes on both sides, so you must be careful not to bump your head.

On the right side (south end), the first thing in sight is a small, iron wood burning stove, dated 1890. It has two open plates on the top surface. Inside the stove are two pairs of shoes, Grandma Webster's tiny button top dress shoes, size four, and Uncle John's black "Sunday" shoes.

Next to the stove sits a rustic gray homemade storage box full of books. The large, black Jones' family Bible, complete with family pictures dating back to the late 1700s or early 1800s, a dog-eared book marking the beginning of the Grange, and two volumes depicting Ohio's part in the Civil War, are just a sample of this box's treasures.

On the floor against the wall are curtain stretchers (complete with nails), bed slats, an old typewriter, an old Monopoly game, and a catcher's mitt.

The bird cage and its stand are next to part of a vanity, with two drawers. On top of the vanity is a metal box filled with buttons. Two boxes on top of a gray storage cabinet contain celluloid dolls and handmade stuffed dolls, including an Amish pair. Behind this are several boxes of canning jars—pints, quarts, and half gallons. Some are blue glass with wire bails and glass lids. The half-gallon tins were used for storing sausage or side meat. The meat was fried down and covered with drippings, then the lids were put on and sealed with sealing wax.

Now comes the orchestra. There are two brass horns, a cherrywood melodeon (dated 1846), four fiddles (including a child's fiddle), and an old record player with dozens of one-sided, heavy records; and best of all, a workable radio. I can almost hear Amos and Andy.

The north side is just as full and just as interesting as the south side.

The first box inside the door contains old dishes. Some date from the late 1800s. The teapot and serving dish have a bunch of grapes on the sides and acorns for handles and lids. The aluminum Christmas tree with its color wheel and the artificial green tree are next to the three electric fans.

Next is an old trunk, lined with wallpaper. This trunk holds my wedding dress, a scrapbook of school days, and homemade birthday, Christmas, and Valentine cards, school year books, old newspapers with historical news, and many other numerous items.

Uncle John's small dome-shaped lidded metal trunk is the most intriguing trunk in the attic. It has small compartments and has been untouched since he died in 1957. He was born in 1874. The trunk contains celluloid collars, cufflinks, love letters, pictures, old paid bills, straight razors, brass knuckles, and a book of remedies on how to cure various ailments. (One remedy for horses included collecting the moss from the south side of a tree before the sun rises.)

During the 1976 Centennial, I added coins and calendars.

There are several boxes of "What-knots" too numerous to name. Far back on the north wall are pretty, woven baskets and one oak middle table leg (which is going to become a candle holder one day).

The next box holds homemade tele-type and copper coil motors. There are three generations of them—Charles Webster, his sons, and his grandsons. The round three-foot high storage container holds photos of people from long ago. They are strangers to me but are still fun to look at. This container also holds wedding licenses, graduation diplomas, baby shoes, someone's hair, more old dishes, bathing suits, straw hats, and more.

Then comes the lard cans and fruit crates. At one time, during World War II, Grandma stored salt and rationed sugar in the attic in these cans. During haymaking time, she sent Uncle John up to get a bag of salt to put on the loose hay to keep it from spoiling. She did not find out until later that he had mistakenly picked up the sugar instead of the salt. The cows, along with the team of horses, Rex and Pearl, appreciated the hay.

There are many old pictures and frames in the attic. The picture I like best is of the Jones' family, ten young adults.

None of them were smiling, Grandma and Uncle John included.

There are antiques hanging on nails and laying on the floor. A bottle capper, brooder lamp, kerosene lamps, potato ricer, rug beater, butter churn, scales, leather straps, wooden ice skates that screw into the soles and heels of your shoes, just to name a few. The arrowheads and other Indian artifacts I found in the fields over the years have recently been added to the keepsakes.

A handmade magazine rack made of tree limbs holds old calendars. There is also the children's electric train set and tracks, Lincoln logs, the iron baby bed and mattress, the baby bottles still in the gift box, and the wicker doll carriage. At one time, there were some crystal dishes with a pineapple pattern. They are now displayed in my cabinet in the dining room.

I can't count how many times I bumped my head on the short doorframe upon leaving the walk-in attic, but that's what it takes to bring me back to the present.

The Covered Wagon

By Donna Mae Webster (1968)

The children were home from school and supper was almost ready. I heard sounds in the distance like trotting horses. But that can't be. Especially not on a paved road in 1968.

We went outside to investigate, and, sure enough, a covered wagon, pulled by two mules, was approaching from the north. It lumbered slowly down State Line Road and pulled up under the "Party Tree" which was a large oak tree close to our house. This is the tree the kids picnic under before heading down to Flatrock Creek to fish.

After talking with the two occupants of the wagon, we discovered that their journey started in Ann Arbor, MI. The destination of the young man and woman was the bottomlands of Kentucky. One of the mules had developed problems with its hoof, and they were headed for the Amish community near Berne, Indiana to trade mules.

I invited them for supper, and they accepted the invitation. Supper consisted of pork chops, mashed potatoes, gravy, a vegetable, peach pie, and homemade bread. Marty almost died of embarrassment when, during the meal, I asked the couple if they were hippies. After supper, Charlie, Marty, and Cindy played music with the young couple for several hours.

During our conversation, we learned that the young woman was an RN and that they were expecting their first child. We invited them to camp in the six-acre woods for the evening. They accepted the invitation.

The next day was Sunday. When we returned home from church, the wagon was gone.

The young couple never disclosed their names, and we never heard from them again. We did, however, learn that they didn't have to trade mules. A pebble was discovered under the shoe and an Amish man fixed it. I'm sure this was a blessing to them since the mules were a matched pair, and they felt bad about the possibility of having to split them up.

The Runaway Mower

By Donna Mae Webster (1993)

The grass had grown so fast in one week that I had to use the leaf sweeper to gather the clippings and dispose of them in the garden. While emptying the sweeper, I left the lawn mower running, in neutral, with the blade off. For some reason, while dumping the third load of clippings, the lawn mower "jumped" into gear and headed west, taking the sweeper with it.

"Please run into a tree or the garage," I thought while chasing the runaway mower. No such luck. The mower made a slight turn to the left and went right through Charlie's garden. Tomatoes and Chinese cabbage were flattened. Now, it was headed southwest—straight for the road, the neighbor's cornfield, and Flatrock Ditch.

John Miller and his sister, Julie, stopped to see what was going on. In the meantime, the lawn mower changed direction again when it hit the ditch by the road. Now, it was headed southeast, through a field of soybeans. I figured it would either go all the way to Van Wert (since I had just filled the gas tank), or, if I got lucky, stop when it got to the woods.

It stopped in the woods. John Miller was following in the forty-four-inch-wide path the mower had made through the soybeans. After he drove the mower back to the house, we discovered the sweeper had been damaged but not beyond repair. Charlie fixed the sweeper, then told me to "Put the mower in the shed!"

"No!"

Again, he told me to put the mower away.

I said, "You like your garden to look nice, and I like my yard to look nice."

So, he retrieved a fork from the barn, and when the sweeper needed dumping, I stayed on the mower while he pitched the clippings.

Is It Magic?

By Martha Webster Rust (1960)

Isn't it magic when the tree leaves bud,
The flowers spring up to reach for the sun,
The birds and planes up so high,
Brooks start flowing and rabbits run?

To see the children running about,
Flying their kites for all to see.
No, it isn't magic, not at all.
God made all these, for you and me.

A Flower's Life

A flower's life is simple.
Its purpose is to provide beauty for all to see.
It is nourished by the fertile soil, the warm sun, and the
gentle rains.
When the nights turn cold and the north winds blow, it
senses the end is near.
It drops its splendid colorful bloom, one petal at a time and
turns inward,
seeking the strength to accept its fate.
With courage and fortitude, it acquiesces to the cycle of
life, knowing that the next time it blossoms, it will be more
glorious than it could ever have imagined.

The Family

(Left to Right) David Eugene, John Charles,
Lucinda Sue, Martha Ann

The Tap Dancer (Angie's Song)

She taps and turns in an endless rhythm.
Never missing a beat,
Dipping, swaying, turning, and stepping,
Aware only of the movement of her feet.

Every pattern weaves a story.
Every step relays
Something that her soul wants to share,
But what is she trying to say?

I try to understand the meaning.
I searched for signs and clues.
But glimpses of reality elude me,
As I'm caught up in watching her shoes.

I feel her weariness. I sense her pain.
But still, she dances on.
I wish that I could stop the music,
But the source cannot be found.

I wonder what force drives her to dance
As I perch on the edge of my seat.
Then, realize that if I'm not careful,
I, too, will start tapping my feet.

The Roller Rink

There's something unique about roller rinks beyond the sweaty smells, the loud music, the aroma of burned popcorn, and sticky floors. It's the only place you can get dizzy without even moving. During the first skating event with the boys, I was stepped on three times, knocked over twice, and fell four times—despite not wearing skates. I was standing on the sidelines with the other mothers.

I remember the first time I took my sons, ages three and five, and my four-year-old nephew skating. I helped the boys get their skates on, which is no simple task. They "put their right foot in and put their right foot out, put their right foot in and shook it all about." Then they hit the floor (literally). They hung onto the handrail along the side and skated their little hearts out. My nephew earned a gold medal for balance. His long coltish legs went in one hundred different directions, but he always caught himself before falling.

Well, the boys worked up quite a sweat. Their hair was dripping wet, they were exhausted, and their feet (and other body parts) hurt. We had been there fifteen minutes!

Many years passed before I took them skating again.

The Telephone

Why did Bell invent the telephone?
I may never really know.
It must have been for physical fitness,
But I couldn't guess it could help you so.

As soon as the phone rings there's a scramble.
An evasion from all over the house.
And if you're not careful, you might be
Kicked, or suffer a tear in your blouse.

Marty thinks it's Denny.
It's only our cousin, Doug.
Disappointedly, she turns around,
And gives me a little tug.

The next time it rings, I answer.
Here comes Marty again.
Turns out it's Aunt Betty.
Disappointment sets in.

Fifteen minutes later, it starts all over,
But this time she didn't run.
I told her it was Denny,
But she said, "You're just having fun."

He called back later and there we went,
Struggling over the phone.
But by the time she said "Hello,"
He'd hung up thinking no one was home.

I guess when Bell invented the telephone
He must have hated the world.
It will lead us to destruction someday.
If it doesn't kill me first!

Scissors for Sister

By Martha Ann Webster Rust (2001)

My sister is a constant friend.
It's just the way it has always been.
She is loving and kind,
Always helping others in a bind.

Sister reaches out to others in need
Reflecting God's love in thought and deed.
She gives of herself without a pause
Never wondering, "Is this a really good cause?"

She expects little in return for all the energy
she doth burn. So, when she turned fifty,
I tried to be nifty and to find that special gift.
Something lasting and special to give her a lift.

She said she wanted nothing.
No surprise party. No fancy thing.
Just a manicure set
or a good pair of scissors to get.

So, I went shopping and shopping.
For something special. I am still looking,
Examining scissors for just the right pair.
There's Fiskars and Ginghers, much to compare.

During a leisurely stroll through an Amish store
Perusing the fabric and patterns galore.
I suddenly spied the scissors that reflect My Sister.
Special, lasting, and perfect.

Pistol Packing Grandmas

By Donna Mae Webster (June 28, 1997)

Iowa Island and Shawnee Shoals were having their annual neighborhood garage sales. The day was bright, hot, and perfectly wonderful for shoppers. Joyce, Mandi, and I had a marvelous time going through other people's junk looking for those unique treasures that we thought were imperative to purchase. Mandy purchased some bottles for the baby due in December. Joyce bought a blouse, and I bought a nylon butterfly.

Around eleven o'clock, we met Charlie and Chad at the Lake George Marina. Chad had to be at work at midnight, so he and Mandi headed back to Van Wert, OH. Joyce, Charlie, and I drove to a few more garage sales then headed back to the campground in Michigan for a meal.

Joyce insisted that we go to more garage sales after the meal. Being an avid flower gardener and knowledgeable about so many plants and their scientific names, she wanted to go to the sale that advertised live plants. She purchased the Cup and Saucer plant that she had been looking for to add to her garden. From there, we were ready to find some more bargains.

The excitement began when we turned the corner of Wright and Cutter Streets. Lying in the middle of the road was a nice jacket. Stopping the truck, Joyce jumped out, picked up the jacket, and was about to hang it on a nail on the light pole, thinking a child may have lost it and someone would come looking for it. The jacket felt so heavy.

At first, she thought there was a walkie-talkie in the pocket. Her eyes got big as saucers as she realized she was holding a pistol.

"What are we going to do?" she asked as she handed the jacket to me.

Holding the jacket with two fingers, I reached into the pocket to see if the pistol was real or if it was a toy. It was real! So now, it has both sets of fingerprints on it, mine and Joyce's.

Answering her question, I said, "To the police station, fast."

We could not remember the location of the police station, so we stopped and asked for directions. It was located next to the fire station.

The vestibule measured five feet by five feet. After ringing the bell for assistance, we talked to the receptionist behind the bullet proof window. Once we told her the jacket had a gun in the pocket, it did not take long for a police officer to come and grab the jacket from us.

Joyce and I were asked to take a seat while the police officer inspected at the gun. We found out it was a loaded nine-millimeter pistol. That upset us.

We asked if they wanted our fingerprints. Laughing at these two great-grandmothers sitting there with worried expressions on their faces, they assured us that fingerprinting wouldn't be necessary. They already had them on the gun.

They took our names, addresses, and phone numbers, and thanked us for finding and delivering the gun to them. It was a scary moment, but we were glad a child had not found the gun, and no one was injured.

UPDATE: July 11, 1997
Two city police officers were eating breakfast in the Garden Restaurant while Charlie and I were there. We told them that three weeks earlier Joyce and I had found a pistol and wondered if the owner had been located. One of the officers told us that the serial number on the gun led them to the owner. He was in the process of moving and had put the gun in his jacket pocket and then laid the jacket on top of his car. He drove off, and when he turned the corner, the jacket slid off. He did not miss it until the police notified him.

Final Thoughts

picture by Charles Barnett Jones (late 1800s)
(great-uncle of Lucinda Webster Hoffman)

The Flowers in Helen's Garden

Helen wanted a flower garden,
So, Luther readied the ground.
Together they planted a beautiful rose
Surprised at the joy they found.

Helen nurtured the rose with tender care,
'Til her back and limbs were sore.
But the rose brought her so much happiness
She decided to plant five more.

She pruned, watered, and fertilized
And kept the weeds away.
She watched over each rose day and night
So, in safety they stayed.

But one Spring Day she noticed
Only five of her roses bloomed.
One had faded quietly away
In the night of Winter's Gloom.

And though she missed the beauty
Of the rose that went away,
She discovered that under its branches
There were three tiny plants to take its place.

It wasn't long before her garden
Bloomed in glorious array.
The aroma filled her senses.
The variety completed her bouquet.

Each flower was treated with special care
And felt her love the same.
They craved her tender touch
As she spoke to them by name.

Ramona, Barbarba, Mark, Joel, Jeffrey, and Arden,
Matthew, Kerry David, Bobby, Barry, and Brad.
And Brian, whose bloom faded much too fast.
Jon and Amy, Joel David, and Chris, Hope,
Angie, Zachary, and Andrew.
Nicholas, Jordan, and Cara—all in the garden grew.

Along came tiny shoots from the flowers already in
place. Kim, Leslie, Alicia, Brandi, Thomas, and Britni,
Austin, JaMarkus, Derricia, and Chase.
And two tiny buds, yet to show their face.

Helen took considerable pride in her garden,
but her tending days are gone.
Now, we need to care for each other
as lovingly as Helen would have done.

Luther and Helen Hoffman
In Loving Memory of Helen Hoffman
May 2, 1917 - March 7, 2000

In Memory of Charles and Donna Webster

Married:

Nov. 25, 1948

Charles Eugene
Webster

Nov. 18, 1928 –

Nov. 16, 1997

Donna Mae Webste

October 26, 1929 – November 15, 2020

Everybody's Mother, Nobody's Child

Donna grew up wondering why her biological parents in Dayton gave her up for adoption at the age of five but kept their other four children. It was a question she often asked both her biological mother, on the rare occasions she saw her, and her adoptive mother, who was her biological cousin, but no answer was ever provided. The question haunted her.

When Donna and Charlie met on a blind date set up by mutual friends, it was love at first sight. After a short dating period (three months) and a Dear John letter to her fiancé, who was serving in the war in Europe, Donna and Charlie were married in the little white church in Dixon, OH. They moved to the Webster farm with Grandma Martha Etta Jones and Uncle John Jones.

I'm sure she was as green as they came, but she would never admit that. Grandma Webster taught her everything she knew about farm life, and it wasn't long before she was milking cows, raising chickens, butchering hogs, driving the tractor, and raising four children. It was a great life centered on church activities with good Christian friends.

It didn't matter your age, whether you were married or single, male or female. She mothered all. "Get your elbows off the table." "Sit up straight." "Look at me when you talk to me." "Don't talk with your mouth full." "Clean up your plate." "Put your dirty dishes in the sink." "Pick up your dirty clothes." "Put your toys away." "Flush the toilet after you use it." And my favorite, "Don't cross your legs with a dress on."

Donna's friendly reminders, parenting and marital advice were given freely. "The World According to Donna" was a short book. There weren't many gray areas. But the black and white of it was sound advice and given with love and the best of intentions.

She had a great capacity for love and forgiveness, saw the good in everyone, and always had an optimistic attitude about life. She spent many years as a caretaker—Uncle John, Great-Grandma Webster, Dad, Aunt Dorothy, Aunt Betty, Aunt Virginia, Uncle Jake—the list goes on. In the nursing home, she served on a committee as an advocate for other residents and held many of her friends' hands as they took their last breaths, offering encouragement and support to their loved ones.

Even through her many illnesses and losses, she kept plugging along. "Just another bump in the road," she would say. She loved a good joke and a good laugh with her boys. She loved outings with her girls. They always had a memorable time.

She was proud of each of her four children, their spouses, her eight grandchildren, twenty-three great-grandchildren, six great-great-grandchildren, two step-grandchildren and five step-great-grandchildren. She would go on and on about how smart and talented we all are and how cute the grandbabies are, because, you know, in the "World According to Donna," it could be no other way.

Donna was a Christian and believed in the resurrecting power of the Holy Spirit through Christ Jesus, her Lord and Savior. We talked about what Heaven would be like and about our new bodies. She wanted a view of cornfields and woods and longer legs that worked. One of her great-granddaughters told her she thought Heaven would be full of hot tubs and never-ending buffets. Donna told her, "Heaven was whatever made us happy."

Donna had a way of making everyone feel at home and welcome. She vowed to give her children the one thing that eluded her, the love of a mother. In that, she succeeded without question.

We pray that after the welcome party is over in Heaven and she gets settled in her new mansion (which will take a while as we all know how much "stuff" she will have to put away) that she will finally get the answer to the burning question "whose child was I?"

I like to think the answer God gives her is the one he's given her for years. "You are MY child, Donna, and that's all that really matters."

One thing I know for sure, we haven't heard the last from her. I can hear my dad asking her, "Ain't that right, Donna?"

I'll Paint You a Sunset

By Donna Mae Webster (1997)

How can I tell you how much I love you and miss you? Words cannot express my emptiness. Yesterday, you were out walking in your garden and laughing with your friends. I walked beside you. Today, I walked alone.

I wish I could tell you happy birthday, but you're not here. And so, I pick up my paintbrush and paint you a sunset to close your day and whisper a cool breeze into existence to refresh you. And I keep on loving you.

I spill moonlight onto your face. It trickles down your cheeks as so many tears have flowed down mine. I want so much to comfort you. In the dawning hour, I'll explode a brilliant sunrise into a glorious morning to show you how much I love you.

I try to say it in the quiet of the green meadow and in the blue of the sky. The wind whispers my love throughout the treetops and spills it into the vibrant colors of the flowers. I shout it to you in the thunder of the great waterfalls and compose love songs for the birds to sing to you.

I warm you with the clothing of my sunshine and perfume the air with nature's sweet scent. And, when the canvas is finished and my paintbrush has made one final stroke, the picture will be of us together again, walking hand in hand in God's Garden, basking in our love for one another, and in God's love for us. Goodnight, my love. Rest well until we meet again.

I Cry for You

By Donna Mae Webster (1997)

My eyes begin to mist,
And teardrops silently fall.
I try to hold them back,
But it's hopeless, after all.

Across the wet eyelashes
Tears flowed down my face.
Sliding down my cheeks
As if each tear is in a race.

At first, they come as droplets,
And then a steady stream.
I try so hard to stop them.
I wish it were a dream.

They started out so tiny,
Transparent as could be.
Nothing can contain them.
My love for you, pouring out from me.

I Have a Name

She sighs deeply as she slides her hands into the warm, sudsy water. It is a welcome respite from a long, busy day.

The canned tomatoes line the countertop, popping as they seal. The sweet corn, cucumbers, and radishes have been gathered and washed. The kids fed, the laundry started, the kitchen mopped, the dairy barn cleaned.

The yard still needs mowed, supper needs started, animals need fed and watered, and the cows need milked again.

She diligently performs her duties each day, fulfilling requirements without complaint or expectation of reward, proceeding with unwavering dedication in a continuous and consistent manner.

Dinner is done, the dishes are washed, the kids are bathed, read to, and tucked in. The laundry folded, the pets fed, the house locked up, the lights out.

She feels the silkiness of her nightie slide over her tired body, promising comfort, no matter how fleeting.

Finally, it's time to rest. Her pillow cradles her head. Her eyes slowly close, her body relaxes.

As she falls asleep, he rolls over and squeezes her breast.

Her response is barely existent. There is no energy left to fulfill one more need. Feeling depleted, exhausted, and drained, she thought, "There isn't much of Cindy left."

Reflections of Me

Her frail body cast a shadow on the wall as she passed through the dining room toward the kitchen.

Her feet shuffled in time with the ticking of the clock on the wall.

Her wrinkled hand grasped the handle of the familiar teapot sitting on the burner.

She turned toward the sink, reaching for the water faucet.

She paused as she saw her reflection in the window.

Who was that aging, grey-haired woman staring back at her?

Her eyes demanded attention. What pain had she experienced? What secrets did they hold? What joys did they savor?

As she turned on the water, she pondered, "Life is but a fleeting whisper in a cacophony of noise. Choose your words wisely."

Life is Short

Life is short, that's what they say.

I never understood what that meant until the day I said goodbye to my mom for the final time.

Regrets, of course.

Memories, the best.

Loss, for sure.

No more "I love you's."

No more advice.

No more unconditional love.

Life is short, that's what they say. Now I understand.

Haven't I Always Told You Where I Was Going?

When you were an infant, and I left you in your bed to get a diaper or a bottle, I always told you where I was going. "Mama's going to get a clean diaper. I'll be right back." "I'm going to warm up your bottle. It will just take a minute." It wasn't long before you knew that I'd be back in a moment, just like I said.

Haven't I always told you where I was going?

When you were a toddler and I had to take out the garbage or throw a load of clothes into the washing machine in the basement, didn't I always tell you where I was going? "You sit here and play. Mama will be right back." You accepted, and even enjoyed, those little moments of freedom from my ever-watchful eye. But you knew I'd be back shortly, just as I said.

Haven't I always told you where I was going?

When you were old enough to stay home by yourself for short periods of time, did you ever have to wonder where I was? "I'm going to run into town and get a gallon of milk. Be right back." "I've got a hair appointment, be back in thirty minutes!" "My meeting should be over by eight." And you acted like you could care less, but I knew you were glad to know where I was and when I would be back.

Haven't I always told you where I was going?

And when you became a teen and I never knew where you were, or what you were doing, you still knew my every move. And if you didn't know where I was or when I was coming home, I was the one who got a lecture. I left you notes on the refrigerator and messages on the machine. You always knew where I was.

Haven't I always told you where I was going?

And even after you made a life of your own, I talked to you each day about my schedule—just in case something happened to you or the grandkids and someone needed to reach me. Now, it seems, the security of having you know where I am is more for me than it is for you.

Haven't I always told you where I was going?

And when I leave you that one last time and tell you I'm going to see you in Heaven—don't be sad. After all,

Haven't I always told you where I was going?